IMAGINING LIVES

Imagining Lives

BERNICE LEVER

 Black Moss
Press

Library and Archives Canada Cataloguing in Publication

Lever, Bernice, 1936-
    Imagining lives / Bernice Lever.

Poems.
ISBN 978-0-88753-500-0

    I. Title.

PS8573.E953I43 2012   C811'.54   C2011-907656-X

Cover image: Marty Gervais

Editing, Design & Layout: Kate Hargreaves

 Black Moss
Press

Published by Black Moss Press at 2450 Byng Road, Windsor, Ontario,
N8W 3E8. Canada. Black Moss books are distributed in Canada and the
U.S. by LitDistCo. All orders should be directed there.

Black Moss would like to acknowledge the generous financial support
from both the Canada Council of the Arts and the Ontario Arts Council.

 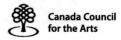

CONTENTS

IMAGINING LIVES

I always listened, tried to imagine
what it was like for Aunt Kay, the Alberta orphan,
taken in for chores—indoors and out—
child labour was free help,
she ate little, stayed small,
—hard leather, buckle boots to struggle into
each day before dawn,
just for her B&B, never for a smile,
once she mis-matched her buckles,
had to redo them under angry glares,
then *"No lunch for you Missy,"*
not even using her name
her duty diary, small, deep-pressed pencilling
getting to name the late spring piglet Tom
knowing she'd eat his pork chops come fall,
still there was handling the newborns
yellow fluffs of chicks,
years grinding by, always asking
to go to school, forever dreaming herself
into a starched white dress and apron
always telling of the local public health
nurse who saved her more than once.

Round bright eyes, high chin,
five feet of practical energy, missing
her younger brother & sister, found decades
later, yet never a child of her own
—just a handful of nieces next door.
No wonder the 'dirty thirties'
were an easy challenge for her.

PRE-PLAY DOUGH

Copying Mother's nimble fingers
my sister and I shaped our mud cookies,
setting each uniform patty
in a sunlit row to bake—
our oven a weathered board
balancing
on two bricks.

We rounded up strong twigs
for cleaning a patch of garden path,
collected handfuls of fine silt,
avoiding the coarse manure-fed patch,
scooped up tiny rain ponds from logs
until our fat fingers could massage
these basic ingredients.
Rabbit droppings were raisins
in those pre-chocolate chip days.

Often we tugged Mom outdoors
to view our backyard creativity.
Once, she caught and paddled me
with her wooden spoon for tasting
our cookie dough. Never learned.

Modern doctors claim earth builds
immune systems, not so sterilized toys.
Guess grandma was right,
"You have to eat a peck of dirt."

GROUNDED

Brown rusty hinges
immobilize old iron steps
this hanging fire escape
creates a midnight entryway
for agile students
or crafty thieves
into this weathered brick dorm

Giggling gals, hoisted
by football dates climb aboard,
gingerly holding
shoes, bare feet silent
on metal rungs, squealing
in beer breaths from cold shivers,
fingers on icy crossbars

(will they escape the fire
of the house mother)
curfew violation
forever grounded

LUNCH WITH
UNCLE THOMAS

He's my Victoria one, the only 'saved one'
with a dozen of 'em—uncles that is—I had to label them
for my own Who's Who. No way to prepare
for the unexpected, just had to visit as having
a full year—my teacher training on the Island.

"Is Bert still on the bottle?"
were first words out of his mouth.
No words of welcome as I step into their parlour.
Least Aunty Anne in her dark checkered
dress shared a limp hug, up the front step.
Now she was silent. Sure enough,
there was a scrawny cot shoved against the wall,
four chairs pushed in, just as Mom had said 'cause
Uncle Thomas, being saved and all,
slept alone, had for years.

His bright, bulging eyes stared me silly;
his words were cough-like spurts, constricted
by his too tight Sunday tie. No handshake even
for me, natch, I paused puzzling for a good answer,
still wanting my lunch, sniffing clam chowder.

"Answer me, girl, a man either carries
        a bottle or a Bible."
"My Dad doesn't take it everywhere,

I mean, not to work."
"Bert's fourth daughter, clever
    with words, just like your sisters.
God will make him pay, you know."

I hoped we'd sit for grace soon;
Aunty Anne had the table laid out
with her flowered china. Cuz was very late,
guess she wanted to skip the sermon.
That was the first time I drank
my coffee black, after seeing Uncle Thomas
lick the drip off the creamer spout.
Thank goodness, for serving the man first.

WOMAN WRASTLIN'

Funny thing is not many women did—
woman wrastlin,' that is: a man's game.
　　　Maybe thar's one pair I heard of—
Douglas sisters: one tall & spare, 'nother one,
short & squat, if'en they'd started into pints
at noon: by nightfall,
one or t'other would kick over her chair,
bellowing 'I ken take ya!'

Down on the scuffed wood floor, they'd
fall, hip to hip, one head to t'other heel,
hips and shoulders flat as can be,
sprayin' beer-soaked curses
'n flailin' legs for a knee lock.

I was only a kid, never saw them two in action,
just men's jokes or bad words,
heard thru' a woven blanket: my bedroom door,
so I peeked; my dad, uncle, t'other buds
rollin' around our lino floor, first in laughter,
jerked out jeers, then into bloody fists—

Usual Saturday night starts, 'bout midnight
beer cut off, 'n into store bought whiskey
or home brew, maybe berry mash;
uncle was a cheerful drunk, swigging a bottle,
stamping bare feet, hootin' n hollerin',
palm slapping his thigh, mouth stuttering sounds,

garbled or foreign or fake words,
  'yee—up, ya—up—up, ieee—up, ta—ta—ieee, ya.'
t'others egging him on, whooping along,
  in his high leaping circle dance, all clapping
own thighs, eying all for a challenge,
then two'em, by some code
I never saw, were a-layin' flat,
side by side on our lino, head to heel,
awaitin' the call: 'Legs up!' A count to three—
two touching hips flicked into action,
legs twisting and bending sideways,
  sweatin' up drops in no time, to lock
  'n knock t'other's back off that floor;

really, it's leg wrastlin,' grew from bein' too
boozed up to sit, chair & table, for arm wrastlin'.
You can't fall from the floor,
always angry shouts 'bout one startin' too soon,
'head of t'count, or some t'other excuse
joined the smoke swirlin' air,
soon spinnin' bodies were into headlocks
or smashin' fists, no longer a laughin' matter
but still a spectacle: like a broken window
'cause we kids didn't have no TV,
and leg wrastlin' was 'n excitin' show.

Yet some Saturday nights weren't fun, white
old guys maskin' their fears, getting
hurt, bouncin' fridges atop bare toes,
just playing macho games.

ANNIVERSARIES

Forget candle light, roses & wine
old fashioned waltzes,
the Victorians are long gone.

Anniversaries are for adversaries
many being antagonistic
going ballistic once a year
an annual anatomy dissection
with rustic discipline,
nailing to the wall
one's faults and failings
open to sadistic evisceration

Anima airs, animal actions
anniversary victims
some survive, none ready
but another one comes 'round.

BIRTH DAY

Celebrate? It might not be a weekend.
You might not be in the mood.

Some aunt is bound to recount
for the umpteenth time
that your gender disappointed,
not what was wanted
so Dad went out on the town,
got drunk and left Mom crying
in the hospital.

What's there to focus on anyway?
This day you mark off another year
from your dwindling supply.

Your cake can't hold that many
candles, your bulging belly can't
hold all the wine you yearn to sip and sip.

Maybe take a detour
on your public declaration
to everyone's calendar,
ignore the unchangeable past;
on such a day, create a birth,
any intriguing idea, a piece of sculpture,
a better political speech,
a finer fuel, any greener mode,
just start something new.

SHADOW PLAY

Shadows play on rain-
filled footprints
ebbing grey splashes
easing away in silver moonlight.

Shadows, my definers,
often my
better half, sweeter
self with blurry
edges, soften me
accept me.

Waning or waxing,
revealing more
than motionless
mirrors.

Shadows fool
me, let me
believe I can shrink
or swell
with dark or light,
easily avoid
constant rigid I.

PLAY DATE

Lil' Em's arranging time, Friday,
to enjoy with Sarah and Sue;
Lil' Em set her own agenda, firm—
dressing up games and giggles;
Lil' Em has three hours to demand
her pals applaud her dreams.

Next week, Lil' Em will obey rules
from supervisor Sue or Sarah
when to laugh, when to clap.

Yet Lil' Emily would rather book
a war afternoon with Jonas and Gerry,
these local heroes have great boxes
of soldiers, jeeps, tanks, flame throwers,
hand grenades and so much more.

Now children are trained to fun
on cue, play no longer
random outbursts,
discovering joy
in the everyday:
  naming clouds,
  skipping stones,
  chasing butterflies

EACH ONE / LOVE ONE

In Remembrance of Martin Luther King Jr.
—April 1968

Citizen Centennial projects
finally over in Canada.
Now—America—set 1968
as stamp-out-hate year.
KING holidays for all slum children.

Every prosperous family share:
bedrooms and bread but
not bullets with your poor.
Let each organization pen a list
for *Operation Vacation.*
Invite them home or you go
homeless, landless, lifeless.

Let ten million—the despairing ones—
enjoy their heritage:
tent over grasslands
splash on every sand grain
forest over the Rockies
fill up the Grand Canyon.
This is your last
summer, America.

Oh, America, the beautiful and damned.
You lack not the means
—you fly troops worldwide—

you lack only the heart.
Let our Canadian prayers operate
your heart transplant.

Love all, America, or watch yourself
ruin in rape and raze
until all is black drape.
If America goes, so does Canada.

OVER

small stinging tears drip
icy wringing fingertips
wedding ring slips off

GOING ON—ALONE

"From Now—On?"

It's good there's no-one there
to witness these old tensions
old bonds, new fear.
from Not Yet but Still
Margaret Avison

It's good to face life's erasers
solo, staring at wind flapping
branches, daring one to snap,
sail down to shrivel, grounded.
Only you at tear-streaked windows,
weather mirroring your woe.
You mutter choices: 'now cremation
fire or embalming beauty' to your
empty, misnamed living room;
it's good there's no one there.

Your racking sobs may jar
loose decade buried images,
even whole video cheering clips
of what may have been your past
entwined, or pastel painted edits
linked by constant change, unhooked
by law but never love; no one
to witness these old tensions.

Each death, for a breath
clarifies our muddled minds
so life's scale dangles unbalanced
lips smile, skin's scent again,
so much yearning, until
angry, balled fists
weigh the opposing side down,
your memories smeared
together once more, recalling
'old bonds, new fear.'

3AM FLAPPING

tired old bird is back
trying to extend her limp wings
flip, flub, flip—
gain altitude,
strenuous lift off
her ledge crumbling

maybe never soar
blue forevers again—
outpace the wind
swoop, glide
using any breeze
to suit her whim

managing a set beat
not too ragged—
in my plump chest
is all we both ask

INCONSIDERATE

There's an elephant
sitting on my heart,
sometimes keeping me
breathlessly alert

just about to give in,
it leaves me gasping

at the last instant
rises up Disney-like
a grey blimp
neon pink mouth agape

me panting shallowly,
lips dry, eyes
giddy with glee

but still its shadow
so near my face
obscures the sun

ever aware of its
inconsiderate returns,
crushing plops.

CLOSED

"A Kept Secret"

Something to weigh until
the branches become black
against the amber evening.
>   from *Not Yet but Still*
>   Margaret Avison

Closed doors, mouths or minds,
shutting away data or dreams,
may harbour what we desire,
even require, kept under lock
something to weigh until

we are floundering in un-
answered pleas or prayers,
stretching hands and hearts
out for bright sunsets as
the branches become black.

Just a ray of compassion, hug
of warm arms, key word
for our puzzling, highlighted
against the amber evening.

IGNORE LINEAR

Minds are beyond machines,
light years away from their maps.

You know what I adore best
about these MRIs
those B&W negatives of my brain:
no straight lines, not even a few
triangles, rhombus or rhomboid
figures shaded 3-D.

Yes, most of all, I adore
those unpredictable curves,
hairpin switchbacks,
crinkly vines, touching digits
in my bumpy, bulging
creviced mind.

No, they were second.
First was that random light show,
impulses still flashing
on and off, then on again.

Just believe, there is more
than zero and one
in your grey matter.

ONE STEP

first one, always the hardest, hands
cupping hip joints, knee bent, lifting
ankle, foot skimming gravel ridges

but a hop, skip and jump sometimes
carry you, overcome timid
'one step at a time'

dry creek or dark crevice
is left far below
maybe even 'high and dry'

when light-hearted feet soar
your wingless body freed
from mud and rubble safely

in feet up, bottom slides
not chancing crashes to shale
or stones scattered underneath

bones snap, not bend to rock
bodies aren't ivies, clinging
vines to another's framework

choose leaping or rolling
whatever works
        whatever saves you

SHOULDER

Jealous of Venus de Milo
desperate for one perfect curve
craving loving caresses
I invite you to drip
your tears—whatever—on my rounded
shoulders; load all your worries
or fantasies aboard.

My back support is available
in many positions, awaiting cues.

SPENT TEARS

There may be no end to love
but the crying stops—eventually
with tears suctioned dry,
moisture only found now
in the slow moving, demanding
heart, dark red and rubbery,
stiffer than bone, slowly hardening
as the weary heart
sucks fluid from every body part:
first from the wet eyes,
wanting only blindness to stop
the sight of anguish for awhile,
then the heart beats stronger
on rich hormone juices
sweet, gooey from the clitoris,
then that excess, too is swallowed
to arid crumbles and wrinkles,
lungs cough with acrid air,
then splutter with too much heart
water from muscle fluids
and joint liquids, as the heart continues
to send commands down arteries,
mining moisture returned by veins,
old ruddy heart even accepting
stomach acid, sour urine and bitter
bile before sucking the brain to silence,
its solidifying muscles to stillness.
Yes, the eyes dry first.

DANCING AWAY

too short, the nights flew starward—
our embrace, the singing beat—
for sunset, for moonrise
for sun-filled daydreams

we jitter-bugged laughing
lungs gasping in band made smoke
we twisted around our spouses
we two-stepped past our children

we danced away our sorrows
our flaws, tasting chocolate lips

your arms were always strong
saving me from teetering into despair
your eyes, smiling
kept me breathing

now empty, silent floors
freeze my feet
and platforms flatten me

I want to be dancing away
joining you in a heavenly waltz

HE KNOWS HOW TO PLEASURE

He knows how to pleasure a woman:
she's arching towards his lips
she's juicy with his touch
as he enjoys moulding
her soft, smooth curves
and the fruits of his labour
and much, much more to savour.

He knows how to pleasure a woman:
limbs curling and caressing
in round and flat places,
mesmerizing with hums and moans
eyes tantalizing with invites
coming surprises, sparking hair,
brief brushing skin,
desperate faster kisses searching
fingers firm
as velvet drapes, nth speed rhythms,
air exhausted sighs,
as sleep begins dreamless,
he knows how to pleasure a woman.

He makes her fit as a fiddle
ready to play his song again.

PRIVATES

Your own billy club bullies
me into submission
not just your wrestling holds
or muscular legs
clamping me still
with your raging eyes
promising pain

your boneless fifth limb
rigid with need or anger
has no personal message
nor private intended gift
just total thrusting invasion
demanding my surrender

RIDE A BUS

If only my thighs would open
wide enough,
mouth ever ready

If only this roof rack
had fingertips pulsing
just a foot apart

If only this roof had duo
stiff rubber cocks
just three feet between,
then most orifices
would be sated

If only for a wild ride
in pelting night rain
over pot-holed mountain
route to ecstasy

If only

STORM QUESTS

"Sultry Day"

Soon there will rise
a sulphur and violet sky.
It will convulse in
fire and water.
                    from *Not Yet but Still?*
                    Margaret Avison

Quickly smog yellow skies
darken to sour thick air
navy and white clouds,
lime and mauve slits appear
boil menacing shapes
blotting up most city light,
soon there will rise,

a roaring, screaming
funnel, our warring weather,
this aiming devil wind from
a sulphur and violet sky.

High rise condo windows shiver,
splinter while trash
flies past intersections,
citizens icy with panic scan
for solid cover wondering where
it will convulse in.

With deafened ears, all race
around flipping bikes, baby strollers,
into cement basements, subways,
asking, "Is this judgment day?"
Electric wires snap, starting bent fingers
hotter than the wailing lashes
of rain, announcing their fears:
city, all gone
in fire and water.

EMERGING FORMS

on Gwen Gray's painting

An English garden maze
sprouting yellow, orange and pink
arms, heads and torsos
as if each pathway were filled
with copulating couples;
such abandon in summer heat haze:
clothes left on porch and patio

these limbs entwine and unwind
in slow, shared rhythms,
not caring if they ever find
their way out of this mystery.

Do not unlock their puzzled pieces.
Let their lust last forever!

ATONEMENT DAY

One day a stone hit
my wrinkly brow,
'I'm guilty, I must make amends.'
but where to begin
so many loose sins?

I'm afraid none will accept
my sorry-faced excuses.
Can my careless carping, greedy fingers,
deliberate damage and sly lies
be reconciled?

Maybe the great Reconciler
can teach me.

DANCE ON THE DAYS

Dance on the days—
    when the fog smothers all
    when the frost climbs the wall
    when the sun blisters flay
    when the moon stays away, you are not alone.

Dance on the days
    when you hear His song,
    the love of the Lord
    holding you strong
    in the crush of crazy times, you are not alone.

Dance on the days
    when all your joints pain
    when your head aches again
    when your eyes grow dim
    when your hopes are slim, you are not alone.

Dance on the days
    when you hear love's music
    when you feel arms' physic
    when you give good deals
    when you share all meals, you are not alone.

Dance on the days
    using your love
    keeping each other
    upright and above
    in the crush of crazy times, you are not alone.

FINDING THE
SURFACE

Breathing in
a water ruled world
vertical sun rays draw
air bubbles to the horizon.

Orange life jackets dot
this ruffling, periwinkle blue
morse code for swimmers.

BETWEEN

Between the stones, grey granites
never two the same colour nor shape
most smaller than a skull or a
fist but sunk into this edging
circling for openings,
walking, avoiding puddles, searching
for a path without tripping yet
cutting our bare feet on sharp chips,
smell of damp earth and sawdust
in this cool drizzle, the sun
blotted enough to be a winter's
moon, carrying on just enough faith
a goad for no retreat
nor surrender, just one muddy
set of toes ahead of the other

Lips too silent to even hum just
dark, sharp spear ends jammed
between smooth river rock and pale
boulders scraped arches
can't stop for a bandaid
heavy canvas backpack locked
on humped shoulders
how many rounds now, seekers?
just that this day is
closing down.

There is no arrival place just
another beginning, repeating
like a modern day Sisyphus, too
confused to learn a lesson or
path, circling, any follower
never wiser, bowed head eagerly staring
for a pattern, a solution in this
rock-edged puzzle,
echoing our breath.

GROWING HOUSE

It all seems so simple at first—
starting: water, sun, a leaf,
once eight centimeter roots
or just dozens of white hairs appear
searching for dirt,
then poof!

Huge silver dappled green leaves
maybe pink floret balls
here and there, contrasting
planting, you add soil,
chemicals.

Suddenly this first creation
in a floor tub is taller than you
stretching upward, filling
your window view.

One night, you shudder awake
ceiling cracked open
rain pouring on your treasures
but plant resists pruning,
has its own mind, straining for moonlight
giant fronds shadow you
        darken all.

'A BIRD IN THE HAND'

What flutters is its heart;

this still pile of beige feathers
'playing dead' on my palm
eyes firmly shut
awaiting

that moment I set down
beyond this too clean window
this stunned swallow

Once rested on cedar railing
catching a tiny breath again
it flies.

If only I could save my own
fledglings so easily
from their 'thorny bushes'
        glass obstacles.

IF A ROCK

If a rock cries out
its garden of boulders snuggle
warmly, comforting each other.

Bordering pond dries its tears
shrub roots nestle it closer
even flowers send scented prayers.

All respond to the anguish
of stone, the defeat
of crumbling, cracking rocks
losing identity
in formless dust.

'A SLIPPERY SLOPE'

A tramp covered in snow
is still a slippery body

Our stiff fingers, well-gloved
slide off his frosted
arms, stiff legs

No corpse loads that stretcher
willingly, never helpful
to us on foot skating ice
knee-deep tripping drifts

Already solid, he's still fighting
avoiding that morgue
      freezer drawer
next to last resting space

ROMAN FEASTS

Romans taught bulimia
as an indoor sport,
gluttony reigning—handy
upchuck troughs lining
their tapestry palace walls
as wine overran goblets,
toga clad bosses keeping
their slaves busy

as do sweatshop owners
with their penny-paid poor
producing the latest robes
and glittering sandals ready
for overstuffed closets,
endlessly consuming—
ignoring the naked hungry.

AUTO CONTROLLER

This shiny concoction of metal and wires,
flashing lights and rubber circles, adjustable
mirrors and seating better suited for a boudoir,
broadcasting tunes and news at random,
even instructs me where to turn
with lessons on parking.

Dear Hal, how dare you take over
my traveling routes, declaring my
destinations, assignations at random?

You force me to keep on the right
side of the streets, even when the beautiful
bodies are on the left, ignoring me.

You shut out bird song and blossom
scent, silencing laughter of strollers,
sealing windows to suit
your level of air conditioning, confining
me to your mechanical hollow.

Please park now, letting
me stroll and pause,
back up or dart sideways
without your auto dominance.

ON RACKS

Metal rungs and restraints, black
rubber bands in consumer displays
customers yearning to feel
lovers gaining painful obedience

The Inquisition racks hidden, rusting
and lonely, in dreary museums

Ask any military commando
for his modern methods
to stretch confession free
from soft, pliable flesh

Words—true or false—
will they satisfy partners, you?

It's just a job: information gathering
news from fear
            data from damage

Torturers and tortured ones
lives intersect in pleas
            in screams, then
                        in fatigue
petit mort or death

AN ISLAND MOURNS

Another graduate partied too well,
wailing is louder than the drumming
from pulsing leather yurts, flailing
with anger, against fear, against death,
now none are well.

The young stride in green woods, wild foxgloves returning
in glory each June, summer repeating its bountiful lessons:
symbols of dotted fawns and songbird chorus
—ignored, June is always a farewell:
some who danced too fast,
some swam in too deep waters,
always edging closer to that exciting abyss
no time for a smiling
'fare thee well'

Some homes, some folks in dark, moon quiet
in thick clouds, the young attack, roaming mountain roads,
screaming and stamping their nightmare now real,
no noise great enough to drown
these images of horror donated in the name of fun.

An island mourns—both the guilty and the innocent forced
to other paths, to believe in arm drooping cedars
smashing dad's car to creative pieces of glass and metal,
teen trapped, lungs drawing in cold creek waters,
blood staining wild flowers, scavenger crows waiting
patiently for the remains of another grad party.

An island mourns—a tent springs up, billowing
larger than any village church,
folks pray harder outside brick walls,
white plastic ripples in sea breezes, snaps
in gusts, attempting to lift the pall.
Coleslaw is plentiful, special brownies, tuna or ham buns,
deviled eggs galore, mourners sipping juice, not booze,
sucking chocolates, awaiting stronger stuff to imbibe alone:
everyone reeks, lost in their loss,
another graduate ground to bottle and bone.

An island mourns: parents, elders shrink
back, huddle together, hush, bend lower,
handing support along the line
to those with empty hands—one less to hold,
ebbing tide rolls shoreline gravel
as the ocean cries its lesson:
graduate.

LEAF DANCING

I saw a leaf dancing, in the sheer joy of lifting, then pausing its sun-tanned fingers, its drying maple shape twisting, turning, side stepping, circling, one side bronze, its twin side golden in flashes with sun through lacy cedar greenery.

Morning rays marked its curving veins, brushing my window sill, then a spiral upward, two twirls, an easy summersault, dip and swing, stasis, next speeding, never repeating in this solo performance, a leaf in love with life, an amazing spirit; thank you, for your minute long rhythm show.

Believe magic, skimming asphalt shingles, just an arm's reach away, constantly flowing, graceful beyond imagining, unbelievably teaching awe, silent creation, giving my heart music, holding me in its spell, rocking, soothing my silly rumbling, tummy fears,

A soft thermal between the green house plant shed and my morning sunlit windows, only alders, cedars and I to watch. Jays and crows unimpressed as the two napping cats.

Unforgettable, now for many minutes, then I walked away, not wanting to see my leaf's swan dive, just left it dancing, nature's mobile art, a ballet of gratitude, turning away from all its fine points and stem still intact, through my picture window .

Then I saw the silken spider's line anchoring this leaf to my eaves, a conductor's wand to the dance of air and leaf. Bravo.

DREAM LODE

decades of data: dates, deadlines, gossip
composting in memory
grey nodes
cut off   drying

cracking synapses
disconnecting from reason: rationality in ashes
sniffing black mold
dissolve into disturbing
dreams: disgorge nightmare riffs.

WILLIAM BLAKE
a poet's North Star

The Mystery is always terrifying,
so Blake used the lion, the tiger, the eagle,
those unknown predators
as bright painted symbols
for his many Christian Londoners
in awe of the vast unseen
so often choose doubtful terror
before embracing the Lamb.

His word pictures and portraits are tongue
pleasing history for us, still yearning
to accept that we are all blessed
as his magical poems now outshine
his copper etched marvels.

CRYING FOR KEATS:
for Love, Beauty, Truth

O, to be Keats' perfect beauty
his unattainable ideal, inspiration
      just within a kiss of our mating
      bursting with awe and lust
totally desirable, his magic
words caressing my ears
      his soft curls upon my cheeks
      cleavage, such sublime

expectant ecstasy is anguish
      knowing he's dying, in truth
      he and his verses can't go on
that I'll never be so in love
not even chosen to act his Fanny.

MUSINGS ON SYLVIA PLATH

a 20th Century Poetic Comet

Why couldn't you wait, Sylvia?
Day dreaming, hoping to meet you,
we were just young mothers
    struggling to find words
for the poems raging inside
    of us—summer of 1963—
household dust, toddlers attached to knees,
hungry husbands, demanding
    our creative energy
as our mouths opened
too often soundless,
just small O's gaping
    dry tongued
    white teeth rimmed
our stilled caves of craving.

LITTLE VOICES
ERODING

Memory murmurs,
niggling, snipping sneers,
brain blasters,
ego implosions

back, recalling schoolyard :
rolling eyes, sniffing noses,
rudely cleared throats

—you can't hit the ball
—you don't have a date
—you won't be allowed
—never you, sorry, no, no

build to vicious voices

—retard, reject, silly
—not unique, dull, hopeless

why try, lie, sigh
hide, hide away, keep silent

no voice, no critics

THERE'S NOTHING SQUARE

There's nothing square
about Robson's rectangle
sunken cement, topless
walls, stairways to waterfalls,
Erickson's wet muse
encouraging city greenery
amid stacked slabs
of glassed-
in offices, but not enough
to nurture poets and painters
to elope beyond
these grey railings
of cubic containers, city-nest control.

PEACE HOLIDAY

Just a clean surface
on everything and everyone
to be noticed and absorbed
as the first time—

be curious anew
thrillingly open to all,
just an hourglass focus of stillness
memory locking wonder,
entering moonrise or waterfall
by choice,
feeling your heart warming
or weeping, truly awake
to living.

WORDS HEARD ON ROBSON AVE.

"Allegation, affidavit," appealed the advocate.
"Which alley? Affie David who?" bleated the prisoner.
"Remand," snorted prosecutor. "Bail denied!" banged the
judge's gavel.
Hearing, jury polling, sentencing, si len cing....
"Did ja see the dancin' trees, gran?"
"My dear, that's Emily Carr's way. She found spirit in
everything."
"Mommy said spirits aren't real."
 "Lady, can you spare a dollar, haven't eaten all..."
"But artist's help us know—" granny's lecturing never pauses.
"Sir, any extra change, today? Bless you."
"Pay me, and I won't even use words," promised the hooker.
Different breaths, separate universes on Robson Street.
Cars stoplighted south on Howe, cars jammed north
on Hornby,
yet traffic swings both East & West on Robson, by
one's choice.
"Gloss, glitter or glimmer," salesgirl's mantra.
"Popsicle pink," giggled the teenie, into wireless images,
not words.
"Orange and poly stripes, so passe,'" sneered penthouse
lady, her diamonds flashing, ordering, "Mixed greens,
sans oil, Pulease!"
Old fashioned book buyers still request
"Atwood, Wayson Choy, Spider Robinson, Crozier,"

as bored generation-Xers, probably younger clerks argue,
"Swank's hot; no, Stones are cool; retro, man, dinosaurs."
Corner guitarists, wanna-be singers share their
unheeded vocabulary with wine connoisseurs, beer
burpers, over-and under-medicated self-talkers, all
jostling for ear space, our memory lane.
Only a fraction of the words heard, English occasionally understood.
Looks & tones, snarls & smiles, body language aids: survival on Robson.

ANYONE LISTENING

Glaring lights blind my dry eyes
as I search
vague shapes shift and merge
move back into blackness

Any opening beyond, some leaving, fan or foe
wafts of dill and garlic increase
          in this jazz cafe

Round edges of a red table
and one empty, plastic chair emerge
from the shadows, mouthing poetry
from this cramped stage.

My halting explanations, alibi-ing
my presence while jangling
keyboard, electric guitar
keep swallowing my words
demanding drums beat my voice
to their rhythms

No one believes my story
Applause signals
my interrogation's over
exit stumbling
   I am invisible
   I am silenced

I AM A CONFERENCE

Can't stop talking nor listening though topics vary, notes get scribbled on margins of programs detailing each hour, the rumours of my days in this lion's lair, so I dare to utter or mutter responses. I opine from supine on my chair, react to speakers who interject, interrupt my thoughts, then constitutional walks with meals down corridors or motions from the floor get seconded or tabled or labelled as cafeteria choices stretch longer than pauses between question and answer sessions, recession, progression, regression, conversation or speech arguing for this method, that approach, some other clause or cause to improve or create an improv which really is the writer's life—a daily recreation, a fiction for another episode of reality.

Why can't I tell the breaks from the sessions? Things are always solved in the coffee line-ups, resolved in washroom chatter, consensus reached at the water fountain for things that matter. Committee of the whole leaves me fractured by the warring factions which issue fissures with diversifying verse or prose that arose from uncommitted statements to mate intentions that were meant or lent to fill the ear while the rear is as numb as the brain is dumb from all this advice, so concise, so applicable to someone who has won the right to write.

I have been conferenced out and about until I am
a conference as I speak as I peek at name tags (not faces
or shoelaces) as identity or status or focus is printed to
be read before I turn red and fall into bed or led into fun
because I do not know your name, just the same, we walk
and talk because after laws, in-laws and outlaws, this is a
conference, and we are meant to confer or bent to infer
from the masses of passes, mounds of messages, messes
of passages, tickets to events and events of the moment,
as pages of papers are considered as monuments or
immaterial, yet made of material, not ethereal as these
voices chanting or ranting at this conference, generating
gas inside and outside of me—a mental morass.